★ ★

FRONTIERSMEN OF AMERICA

Buffalo Bill
OF THE WILD WEST

MATTHEW G. GRANT

Illustrated by John Keely and Dick Brude

D1709453

GALLERY OF GREAT AMERICANS SERIES

★ ★

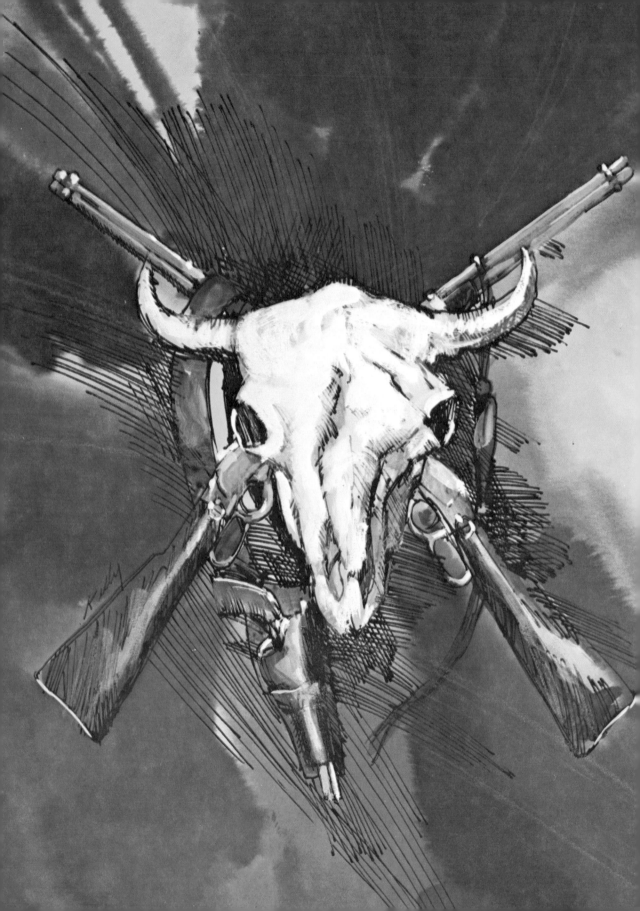

Buffalo Bill
OF THE WILD WEST

Library of Congress Number: 73-10073   ISBN: 0-87191-255-4

Published by Creative Education, Mankato, Minnesota 56001

Library of Congress Cataloging in Publication Data
Grant, Matthew G.
  Buffalo Bill of the Wild West.
              (Gallery of great Americans)
  SUMMARY: A brief biography of the frontiersman whose many careers during a lifetime of ups and downs included Pony Express rider, Indian fighter, scout, and star of the Wild West Show.
  1. Cody, William Frederick, 1846-1917—Juvenile literature. [1. Cody, William Frederick, 1846-1917. 2. The West—Biography] I. Title. F594.C6817 978'.02'0924 [B] [92] 73-10073
ISBN 0-87191-255-4

CONTENTS

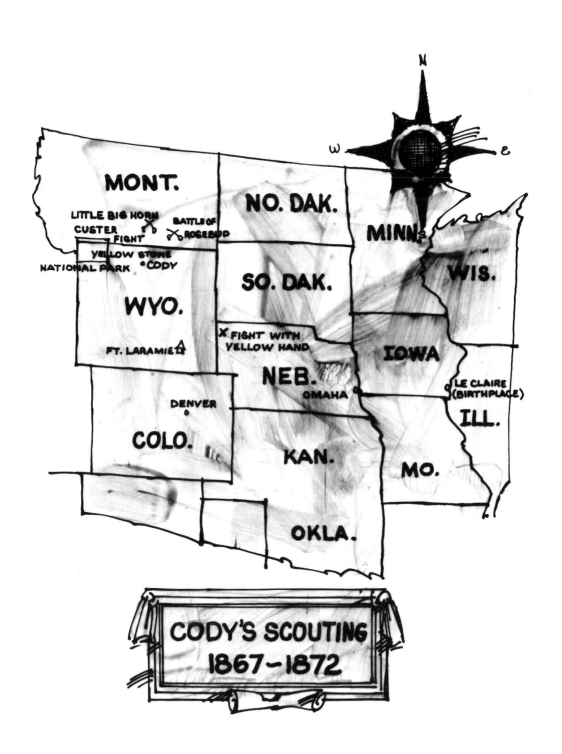

N

W   E

MONT.

LITTLE BIG HORN
CUSTER   BATTLE OF
    FIGHT   ROSEBUD

YELLOW STONE
NATIONAL PARK   CODY

WYO.

FT. LARAMIE

NO. DAK.

MINN.

WIS.

SO. DAK.

X FIGHT WITH
YELLOW HAND

IOWA

NEB.
OMAHA

LE CLAIRE
(BIRTHPLACE)

DENVER

ILL.

COLO.

KAN.

MO.

OKLA.

CODY'S SCOUTING
1867-1872

A BOY ON THE PLAINS

William Cody spent his boyhood on the wild Kansas plains. In 1857, when he was eleven, his father died. He went to work on a wagon-train to support his mother and young sisters.

He could ride like a man, and he earned a man's pay. One night on the trail, an Indian crept up on camp. Young Will Cody shot the brave. The admiring wagon-men spread the story far and wide. Will was called "the youngest Indian-slayer on the Plains."

At Fort Laramie, Will met Kit Carson and Jim Bridger. They became his friends.

Carson and Bridger taught the boy how to survive in the wilderness. From them he learned the arts of tracking and pathfinding. He learned Indian ways and sign-language.

His mother made him go to school for three months. He just barely learned reading and writing—then ran away to the Plains again. He hungered for a different kind of education.

During the next few years he trapped beaver and prospected for gold. When he was 14, he rode for the Pony express, carrying mail in a pouch through hostile Indian territory.

When Indians stole Express horses, Will went off with a band of men and helped shoot up a helpless Cheyenne village. He saw nothing wrong in "teaching redskins a lesson."

One of his friends was James Butler Hickok—later known as Wild Bill. The two rode together, fought together—and even drank together. Even as a young boy, Will Cody was fond of firewater. This weakness would get him into deep trouble later in life.

During the Civil War, he served as a scout. In 1866, he married Louisa Frederici.

A LEGEND IS BORN

For awhile, Will tried to run a hotel. But he longed to be back in the midst of excitement. Hickok convinced him to go back to scouting. The great Indian Wars were beginning in the West.

Will served with Colonel George Custer's Seventh Cavalry and also with the Tenth Cavalry, a regiment of black troopers. He was so good at his job that he earned a colonel's pay. Later, he called himself "Colonel Cody" because of it!

Then he tried to sell land to settlers. But he was a failure. To support his family, he became a buffalo-hunter for the railroad.

Meat was needed for the workers building the Kansas Pacific. Will Cody, age 22, killed some 4,000 of the great animals in 18 months. Because of him and other white hunters, buffalo began to disappear from the Great Plains.

The Indians saw their main food supply disappearing. Whites made treaties with them —then broke them. The red men fought back.

DIME NOVELS AND DUDE HUNTERS

Cody served as an army scout again. One general said: "He is the best white trailer I ever saw." He got in trouble because of drinking, but army officers forgave him because he was brave.

In 1869 a stranger came to the fort where Will Cody was staying. He was Edward Judson, who wrote dime novels under the name "Ned Buntline." The writer was looking for a hero he could exploit in his "true" stories of the West.

Will told Ned Buntline exciting stories of his adventures. Later that year, people read Buffalo Bill: The King of the Border Men.

A lot of Buntline's story was faked. But people in those days only wanted action. They weren't looking for sober truth. They read about "Buffalo Bill" and loved him. Will took

up his new name and new fame gladly. Being admired agreed with him very well!

He soon found a way to profit by his fame: he became the first dude rancher.

Parties of wealthy men began to come into the West, looking for excitement. Buffalo Bill guided them and helped them to shoot wild game. In 1871 he was so famous that he guided the Grand Duke Alexis of Russia, son of the Czar. Buffalo Bill's fame spread from America to Europe. And the dime novels about his imaginary "adventures" were snapped up by the reading public.

The Indians grew more and more desperate during the 1870's. They were being pressed into dreary reservations, their ancient hunting lands taken over by whites.

Buffalo Bill was called back to be Chief Scout for the Third Cavalry. In 1873 he led an attack on the Sioux and was given the Congressional Medal of Honor.

Ned Buntline persuaded Buffalo Bill to enter show business. He played himself in amateurish action dramas—and audiences liked him! Wild Bill Hickok and some of Bill's buddies joined the show. By 1876, they were making a fair amount of money.

Then Bill's old friend Custer was killed

at the Battle of Little Big Horn.

"I'll avenge him!" cried Buffalo Bill.

THE WILD WEST SHOW

He guided the Fifth Cavalry as they attacked the Cheyenne. He fought Chief Yellow Hand in a famous duel and killed him. Then he cried: "The first scalp for Custer!"

When he returned to show business, people thronged to see him. He bought a large cattle ranch with his earnings.

In 1883 he presented his first outdoor

show in Omaha. It was a success and the start of his Wild West Show. This grew into a combination rodeo and circus. It featured trick riders, Indian "attacks," and plenty of gun-play.

Annie Oakley, the top woman sharp-shooter, joined the show. So—for a short time—did Chief Sitting Bull, the Sioux leader who had defeated Custer at the Battle of Little Big Horn.

The Wild West Show went to England, where it played before Queen Victoria. She loved it. It was a success everywhere and Buffalo Bill made and spent millions during the next 15 years.

Then good fortune left him. A train crash destroyed part of the show. Cody drank heavily. Rival circuses stole away his audiences. Buffalo Bill went on for another 15 years, going slowly downhill but game to the last.

He died in 1917. His greatest memorial is the Buffalo Bill Museum in Cody, Wyoming —a city he had helped to found.

★ ★

GALLERY OF GREAT AMERICANS SERIES

★ ★

INDIANS OF AMERICA
GERONIMO
CRAZY HORSE
CHIEF JOSEPH
PONTIAC
SQUANTO
OSCEOLA

EXPLORERS OF AMERICA
COLUMBUS
LEIF ERICSON
DeSOTO
LEWIS AND CLARK
CHAMPLAIN
CORONADO

FRONTIERSMEN OF AMERICA
DANIEL BOONE
BUFFALO BILL
JIM BRIDGER
FRANCIS MARION
DAVY CROCKETT
KIT CARSON

WAR HEROES OF AMERICA
JOHN PAUL JONES
PAUL REVERE
ROBERT E. LEE
ULYSSES S. GRANT
SAM HOUSTON
LAFAYETTE

WOMEN OF AMERICA
CLARA BARTON
JANE ADDAMS
ELIZABETH BLACKWELL
HARRIET TUBMAN
SUSAN B. ANTHONY
DOLLEY MADISON

★ ★